THE EFFICIENCY BLUEPRINT

12 PRINCIPLES FOR LIFE TRANSFORMATION

SELF DISCPLINE IS THE FOUNDATION OF CONTROL

JAMES HARDY

MR.COLORADO

The Efficiency Blueprint

12 Principles for Life Transformation

First published by Key Unity LLC 2023

Copyright © 2023 by Mr.Colorado

All rights reserved. No part of this publication may be reproduced, stored or transmitted in any form or by any means, electronic, mechanical, photocopying, recording, scanning, or otherwise without written permission from the publisher. It is illegal to copy this book, post it to a website, or distribute it by any other means without permission.

Mr.Colorado asserts the moral right to be identified as the author of this work.

Mr.Colorado has no responsibility for the persistence or accuracy of URLs for external or third-party Internet Websites referred to in this publication and does not guarantee that any content on such Websites is, or will remain, accurate or appropriate.

First edition

ISBN: 979-8-218-26412-3

Cover art by Mr.Colorado
Editing by Mr.Colorado
Illustration by Mr.Colorado

This book was professionally typeset on Reedsy.
Find out more at reedsy.com

It starts and ends with you. You must be able to channel the inner god for ultimate empowerment.

James Hardy

Contents

Preface ... ii
1. Don't be a Master of Nothing ... 1
2. What's More Important? ... 9
3. Laziness is a Sin ... 20
4. It's a Lifestyle, not a Diet ... 24
5. Never Do It Just to Do It ... 37
6. I Don't Have Problems ... 43
7. Experience Everything ... 49
8. When You Spend You Lose ... 52
9. Wealthy Before Money ... 54
10. It's a Journey ... 57
11. Pay Attention to What Pays ... 61
12. Stop Doing too Much ... 64

Final Words ... 66
About the Author ... 68

Preface

Before we get started, the first principle for anything is to just get started. Ready to escape the "normal" life and achieve the vibrant life you desire? I offer you the culmination of a quarter-century of experience. This transformative guide will propel you towards a life beyond your wildest imagination just by forming efficient habits.

I have distilled the essence of success into a robust framework that will create discipline and efficiency in your life. Every chapter is infused with the wisdom of 40 books that have shaped my journey, as well as the invaluable guidance of my mentor, who propelled my growth beyond measure in just three short years. Shout out to B. she exposed me to the beauty of journalism and my peers that also published books. Shout out to Austin B. for the motivation for the illustration in chapter 12. Finally, a special shout to my mother, family, and friends for the love and encouragement.

This is not just a memoir; it's a treasure trove of actionable lifestyle changes you can immediately apply. I crafted this gem to bring you the blueprint to achieve your dream life, a life of abundance, joy, and total control over your time and destiny.

Efficiency is the golden key to unlocking your full potential.

So, if you seek a life of purpose and prosperity, this book is your ticket to success. Don't miss this opportunity to grasp the principles that will supercharge your life and set you on a trajectory toward greatness. Join me in this empowering adventure, and let's usher in a new era of extraordinary achievements together. This book is written in the perspective of a young African American male in America.

If you don't like to read there's a quote and a illustration at the end of each chapter.

1

Don't be a Master of Nothing

Master Yourself to Understand Everything

- Frequently in life, individuals find themselves uncertain about their aspirations or the rationale behind their actions due to an unfamiliarity with their own selves.
- If you keep making the same mistake in life, people consider you dumb. But there's likely a more profound issue; you must dig into yourself, your history, or your environment to identify why you keep making the same mistake.
- Why would you fight a bear without a weapon? Most logical people wouldn't because they understand that a bear is more ferocious than a human.
- If you're good at cooking and like cooking, then doesn't it make sense to cook food and sell it?
- If you like warm weather, doesn't it make sense to live in a warm state?
- These are self-explanatory examples of a very vital principle. Learn and fully understand yourself before trying to learn

or understand anything or anyone else.

History

Before you know who you are, you must know where you come from and how you and your family got to this present-day state.

- Understanding how the society that you live in was formed and how it operates allows you to understand how you fit into it.
- Study the values and principles of your successful and revolutionary ancestors first, then take their best traits and apply them to your life.
- Study your ancestors who fell into the trap and understand why they fell into the trap.
- Analyzing your history broadens your perspective and gives you a different point of view.
- Finally, use your history as a tool to empower yourself.
- For example, as an African American male living in America, I realized that my people are so powerful that tactics have been and are constantly used to hinder our growth as a unit. That helped me achieve a superior level of confidence to understand that the majority of the oppression now in America comes from the mind.

Origin of Oppression

I started with how my ancestors originally got to America and how forms of oppression are still in place today. I leave out many details, but I just want to go through the thought process of some questions I had to ask to gain a better understanding of my family and I.

How did I get to America?

- Starting off, Caucasians stole Africans from their peaceful homes and killed the ones that rebelled to enslave them in America. Once enslaved, they hid and destroyed their history and language. When you hide someone's history, they no longer know who they are. If you don't know who you are, you become lost. Once you're lost, you allow others to dictate who you are. When you are lost, you live with no purpose or self-awareness.

What are the reasons why my dad could have gotten hooked on drugs?

- Caucasians flooded minority neighborhoods with drugs; once you take someone's mind from them, you destroy them. You eliminate the family element once you take a parent out of the home with using or selling drugs.

Why was I raised to believe I'm only an athlete?

- Without a father figure inside the home, young men and women are forced to seek external male leaders. Mainstream media historically only promotes derogatory news about black people, such as constantly highlighting crime, glorifying musicians, athletes, and entertainers without glorifying successful black people in other industries, limiting a child's mind because they believe they can only do those few things in life.

What are the current oppression tactics?

- Current and more recent tactics include:
- Banks did not lend to blacks to buy homes, especially in certain areas.
- Venture capitalist firms currently lend very small amounts of money to black start-up companies compared to the overall percentage of money given.
- Prosperous black communities have been destroyed through hate crimes and other tactics.
- There are many employment discrimination tactics. Such as discrimination of candidates with "black names."
- They currently use tactics to intentionally feminize the male figure. Creating feminine men and masculine women. Which can potentially prevent African Americans from carrying on our legacy if males aren't reproducing with women at the same rate.

All of this is relevant because you will forever be oppressed when you don't know who you are. Not knowing who you are will result in a melanated person walking around with sunscreen on their skin. Not understanding the cancer-causing chemicals used to make sunscreen or the fact that it isn't logical to block the health benefits of the sun. The highest level of oppression is to remove a group of people's identity from them because if you don't know who you are, you accept everything because you think it's "normal."

Prosperity

Many of us as African Americans don't know who we are or where we come from, and that's by design. So, once you study some of your history and understand how you got to this moment, now it's time to focus on growing and building from this point. So let's use history to create confidence.

- Starting with ancient African civilizations that were prominent and dominant for thousands of years, creating highly efficient systems. This empowered me knowing that my ancestors were originally kings and queens.
- Nat Turner formed a successful slave rebellion in 1831. Following this rebellion, stricter laws were passed against African Americans, preventing them from gathering in groups. I use this story as confirmation that we are stronger together, so when we build together, we accomplish more.
- Then the underground railroad was formed, where freed blacks helped enslaved blacks escape from slavery. This helped me understand that once we are able to identify the oppression, we are able to fight it.
- Booker T. Washington encouraged African Americans to focus on educating themselves to improve their own circumstances as opposed to focusing on racial equality. Which helped me understand that it's more important to better myself than focus on having rights in a country that enslaved my people.
- Marcus Garvey founded the Universal Negro Improvement Association (UNIA). He issued shares in his companies. He influenced millions of followers with his goal to get blacks back to Africa. I admire him for his leadership and business

skills.
- Malcolm X encouraged African Americans to protect themselves by any means from white hate crimes; he believed that every African American has god within them; and finally, he highlighted the benefits of separation. I have the highest regard for Malcolm X.
- The Nation of Islam is a very strategic and empowering organization that promotes discipline and black nationalism. Analyzing the NOI helped me change my perspective on myself.

This is a small part of our history, but studying powerful people allows you to unleash a superior level of confidence. As well as a strong sense of pride to embrace who you are and know that you are mighty and can't be stopped.

How to learn about yourself

You must start by escaping from the external world's influences and channeling your inner god or self. The outside world—family, friends, school, social media, and news—influences our beliefs based on our religion, perception of the world, race, and ourselves. We never fully develop our unique thoughts, which stops us from exploring the world in our most authentic form.

1. Spend time alone through meditation, walks, and journaling.
2. Get off social media and develop your own thoughts.
3. Stop watching TV. Television is called TV programming, which is used to manipulate the mind. When you see something so much, you start to believe it.

4. Keep trying new experiences. Notice how each activity makes you feel to find your interests.
  5. Constantly self-reflect through journaling, personality tests, receiving feedback, understanding strengths and weaknesses, etc.

Self-Awareness

  1. Who are you? How could you ever authentically be yourself without understanding who you indeed are?
  2. You must understand who you are to know what you want.
  3. Understand your history and study your parents to learn where some of your habits derive from.
  4. To find true fulfillment in your life, you must understand what makes you happy, what brings you peace, and what makes you feel uncomfortable.
  5. To effectively grow, you must know your strengths and weaknesses.
  6. Being self-aware allows you to constantly build your relationships because it's easier for you to communicate your values and boundaries.
  7. Self-awareness improves your decision-making because you know exactly what you want.

Purpose

The ultimate goal is to continue and build your culture, race, or tribe so the generations behind you are put in a position to extend far beyond your imagination. Everyone was placed here for a reason; we all have a special calling or gift to share with the world. To find that gift, you must know your purpose.

Finding your purpose is very challenging. People go their whole lives without ever finding their true purpose. But most people never disconnect from the outside world long enough to intrinsically find themselves. Finding your purpose is simpler than people realize; it is just understanding your values and strengths.

The obstacle hindering people from manifesting their desired life isn't typically time or resources; it's often rooted in a lack of direction, focus, and motivation. Maintaining the drive required to achieve your aspirations becomes an uphill battle without a clear grasp of your purpose.

Why does it matter?

"Knowledge of self is the foundation of living an efficient life."
James Hardy

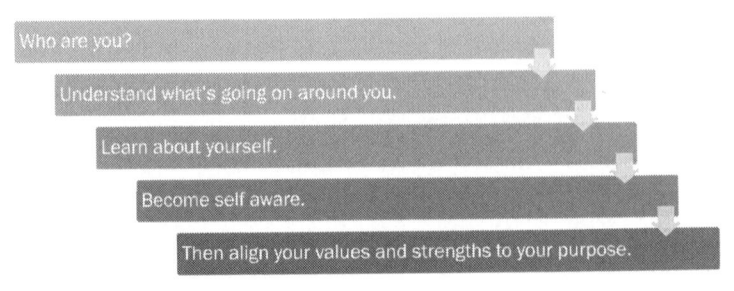

- Who are you?
- Understand what's going on around you.
- Learn about yourself.
- Become self aware.
- Then align your values and strengths to your purpose.

Master Yourself to Find your purpose

2

What's More Important?

Never Sacrifice Your Health

- Every single decision you make in life, make sure that health is your priority.
- Health embodies a holistic equilibrium encompassing the Mind, Body, and Soul.
- The term "healthy" is measured by quality of life. Usually, people don't realize they're unhealthy until they are sick, or their quality of life is compared to another individual.
- The better your health, the more valuable you are because you can be the best version of yourself.
- The purpose of being healthy is to prevent diseases and sickness before they arise by preparing your immune system to be in its optimal state to fight any infection.
- Our health is the only thing in life that we fully control. Therefore, it's in our best interest to maintain a high-quality lifestyle.

Mind:

The power of the mind is limitless as long as we position the mind to perform at its highest capabilities.

- To keep the mind at its highest state, it must be fed the highest quality foods and put in the best environment to thrive.
- An overall healthy diet is essential to maintaining health. But there are specific foods that offer nutrients specifically to protect the brain and help it thrive.
- Sleep is a necessity to restore the brain's energy.
- It's easier to be positive when you're around positive people and viewing positive content.
- Learning is the primary way to improve cognitive abilities.

Diet:

An overall healthy diet is essential to maintaining optimal health. Nonetheless, there are specific foods that offer superior benefits to protect the brain and help it thrive.

- Omega-3 fatty acids improve brain health and development. These foods include walnuts, avocados, flax seeds, and chia seeds.
- Vitamin B9 increases the production of neurotransmitters. These foods include leafy greens and legumes (Beans).
- Antioxidants help protect the brain from oxidative stress caused by free radicals. These foods include berries and colorful vegetables.
- Magnesium is vital high levels of magnesium in the brain

are shown to prevent and reduce fatigue, anxiety, and depression. This food includes leafy greens, pumpkin seeds, chia seeds, and hemp seeds.

Sleep

Sleep is the body's time to reset and rejuvenate. Getting an adequate amount of sleep with a consistent sleep schedule leads to enhanced cognitive function.

- It's vital to set up your life to ensure you can maintain a consistent sleep schedule.
- Getting a full night of sleep allows your body to experience all of the necessary stages of sleep to restore the body's energy levels.
- Full nights of sleep improve and stabilize emotional well-being. Without adequate sleep, people increase their chances of experiencing anxiety, irritability, and stress.

Positivity

There are no benefits to being negative. But how could you not be negative when you consume harmful content and low-vibration foods?

- Surrounding yourself with positive people improves your mood and allows your brain to operate in an efficient state.
- When you choose to immerse your mind in positive content, you efficiently protect your mind from entertaining negative thoughts.
- Focus on being grateful. The easiest thing we can all do is

say thank you for one thing each day. You can show your gratitude through journaling or by expressing yourself to others.

Learning

The most essential part of maintaining and improving brain health is to continue to learn.

- Learning is like exercise for your brain. Cognitive function can't improve without learning.
- Always challenge your brain in different ways to keep your mind active. Activities: Reading, learning new skills, solving puzzles, escape rooms, gaining certifications, etc.

Body

Our physical appearance, or physique, is our initial impression on others, so prioritize shaping and maintaining your body to its utmost potential.

- Please don't be lazy; you can tell when a person is lazy with their body.
- Strength training not only strengthens our muscles but also improves bone health.
- Cardio is a must to reduce fat and improve heart health.
- Stretching is essential for flexibility, which improves balance and prevents injuries.
- Exercise improves physical health, reduces stress, and promotes longevity.

Strength Training

Strength training can be achieved in many ways; besides muscle growth, it boosts physical health. Many people limit their exercise routine to just one form of weightlifting, but there are many ways to improve strength.

- Resistance Training: This form of training builds strength by creating resistance for your muscles. Workouts: planks and wall sits.
- Olympic Weightlifting: Focuses on explosion and power. Workouts: hang snatches and clean & Jerk.
- Circuit Training: This combines strength training and cardiovascular exercise. Performing multiple exercises in a fast-paced environment.
- Calisthenics: Exercises consist of a variety of body weight movements. Workouts: burpees, plank varieties, pull-up exercises

Cardio

Cardiovascular exercises are designed to improve heart health and reduce fat. I look at cardio as a time to free my mind, not as a workout.

- The most common type of cardio exercise is running. Running in nature is natural as opposed to running inside a confined space.
- Bike riding is another type of cardio training. If you don't have a bike, when you travel to mountain regions or beaches, there are plenty of bike rentals.

- Swimming has been considered the best workout by many throughout history because it's a full-body workout that's easy on the joints.
- Jump roping is common for boxers, but adding it to your workout regime is essential.
- Dancing is a great form even though it's usually looked over by many, but zumba, salsa, and twerking classes for women are all great options.

Stretching

Stretching is another important aspect of keeping the body in its highest state. The Benefits of stretching include:

- Improving flexibility is the range of motion in your joints and muscles. It improves joint health, reducing the risk of degenerative conditions as you age.
- The increased elasticity of the tissues reduces the likelihood of strains or sprains. This lowers the risk of injury.
- It promotes blood flow to reduce stiffness, reducing the time your muscles recover from being worked, creating a speedy recovery.
- It improves your posture by relaxing and lengthening tight muscles and promoting better alignment.

Soul

Spirituality is connecting with yourself, nature, and a higher power.

- A spirit-guided mind paves the path to peace and vitality,

while a mind driven by the flesh heads towards death. Which means you shouldn't fall into worldly temptations.
- Mediation helps us connect to our higher selves through controlled breathing, increased self-awareness, and allowing ourselves to escape from the external and fully tap into our inner selves.
- Journaling is vital for reflection. This allows you to gain a deeper understanding of yourself.
- We are nature; we come from nature and need nature to operate at our maximum capacity.
- Crystals are naturally occurring minerals from the earth used for their energy properties. Crystals give off different frequencies, which we can use to influence our energy, help us manifest, and heal us.
- Honor your ancestors; they are an extension of yourself. All of their contributions directed us to this exact moment.

Mediation

Mediation is used for connection.

- To meditate, find a quiet and peaceful place. When you meditate, the goal is to remove yourself from the external world. It's your option to mediate in silence, with a frequency, or through guided mediation.
- Higher Self: Mediation allows you to gain a greater sense of self, and stillness enables you to listen to the god that lies within.
- Consciousness: A heightened level of awareness allows our mind to surpass conventional ways of thinking.
- Presence: People spend too much time worrying about

the past and thinking about the future, never enjoying the present. Living in the present reduces anxiety and increases happiness by allowing yourself to fully enjoy the moment.

Journaling

Journaling allows us to reflect. Through repetition, you gain knowledge and understanding.

- Self-Discovery: Gives you the opportunity to vent and express yourself, which helps you gain a deeper understanding of yourself.
- Creativity: The more you can write down your ideas and track them, the more you can build on each idea to expand and grow creativity.
- Reflection: Journaling allows you to capture and remember memories in detail.
- Goals: Every successful person keeps track of their goals. Journaling gives you a place to monitor and keep track of each goal. As well as turning each idea into a reality, setting a goal, and making a plan. Then you can never fail.

Nature

We are one with nature; the closer you're with nature, the more in tune you're with yourself.

- This fast-paced city lifestyle can create a sense of busyness and leave people feeling overwhelmed, as opposed to spending time in nature, which offers a serene escape from the city's "chaos," allowing us to find solitude and a chance to

recharge mentally.
- The natural harmony of life is how Africans lived for thousands of years; it was never interrupted until Caucasians came and removed our ancestors from their peaceful living.
- Achieving authentic self-understanding and optimal well-being requires embracing our inherent connection with nature, as it provides the essential foundation for our holistic health.
- Spending time in nature, using nature to heal yourself, using natural products instead of chemicals for our hair and skin, and eating in-season local organic produce is the best way to fully tap into nature.
- Anything that goes against the laws of nature isn't good for us. Go into the wilderness alone and observe the peace and freedom you feel.
- There are people who live in Denver but never go to the mountains. Imagine being so trapped that you never experience anything outside your regular routine.

Crystals

Crystals are potent energy sources harnessed for various purposes, and their inherent energy properties bring various benefits that positively impact every aspect of our lives.

- Crystals are used to interact with the energy fields of the body and the energy fields around us.
- The crystals are used to cleanse and purify our energy and the energy around us, protect us, and remove any negative energy we encounter.
- Crystals help to enhance manifestation. Manifestation is

vital when setting and achieving goals. Once you visualize yourself living that goal, it becomes 10 times easier to achieve that goal.
- Crystals are a tool to balance our emotions. They help relieve stress or give us confidence when needed.
- Wear crystals, bathe with crystals, sleep with crystals, meditate with crystals—incorporate crystals wherever possible.

Ancestors

We must pay tribute to our parents, mentors, elders, grandparents, and any older person who paved that way.

- Caucasians had to destroy our history to control us; if they had allowed us to know our power, they couldn't have enslaved us.
- The more we know about our history, the better we understand ourselves.
- Our ancestors are an extension of us. They are us, and we are them.
- The goal is to continue the legacy and grow and invest in your last name.
- By valuing our ancestors, we lay the foundation for future generations to do the same.
- If someone doesn't know their lineage, they can't take pride in the lineage. Without that connection to your roots, you will forever be lost. Constantly searching.

Why Does it Matter?

"Without understanding the importance of health, you can never build wealth. Delayed gratification is the key to being healthy and wealthy." - James Hardy

- Imagine going your whole life without experiencing how it feels to be in optimal health? Health is our most valuable asset.
- The healthier you are, the more energy you have to accomplish your goals.

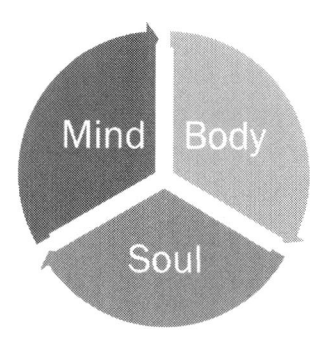

Holistic Health

3

Laziness is a Sin

To Waste Time is to Waste Life

- Every single second of every day of every year is an opportunity to grow and maximize our full potential.
- We must use our time with grace. We must be graceful with our time. Maximizing our time allows us to experience more of life.
- Laziness is for the weak. A lazy person is a defeated person because no one has to defeat that person; they've already defeated themselves.
- Having a schedule is essential for a productive life. The more effective you are, the more you accomplish. Being able to handle everything you need to complete, plus having time to enjoy recreational activities, is freedom.
- The more productive you are, the more efficient your life is. The more efficient your life is, the more freedom you have.
- To waste time is to destroy life.

Time

Value time more than anything else; time is the only thing that we can't get back.

- Therefore, take your time very seriously. As an efficient person, measuring your ROI for every second spent is mandatory.
- The goal is to spend as much time doing the things you value and as little time as possible to make the most money possible.
- There's a work-life balance as well as a time-money balance.
- This means before you pay for any service, ask yourself. "Can I do it myself, or is there an alternative to solve this problem, and what provides the best return?"
- You usually have two options. Save money by doing it yourself or paying for convenience.
- Then you factor in whether spending time doing this task makes sense or spending money but saving time.
- Prioritize tasks each day what's the most critical task and the most efficient way to complete that task?
- Analyze how you spend every single second of the day, cut out waste, and adjust your approach accordingly.

Routine Even During Chaos

What separates a highly efficient person from an average person is maintaining a routine when their schedule is disrupted.

- Having a schedule puts you in a position to accomplish

everything you desire.
- Two effective methods to accomplish your necessary tasks every day, regardless of the circumstances.
- Develop an "I'm going to finish this regardless today" mentality. Understand that there's enough time every day to handle every task. If not, you must remove or reduce distractions.
- If you're more productive during a particular time of the day, prioritize the most critical tasks. For example, if you know you're more creative in the morning, then focus that time on developing your ideas, working out, focusing on your business, or whatever is the highest priority at that time in your life.

Why Does it Matter?

"Every efficient person understands time management. The goal is to create a perfect work life balance that allows financially stability and freedom to do what you want whenever you want."
- James Hardy

- Being resourceful with your time and money lead to wealth.

Time + Money = Wealth

Time Efficiency

4

It's a Lifestyle, not a Diet

Healthy Lifestyle

- The goal is to live an all-around healthy lifestyle. When you live according to the laws of nature, you will always be in optimal health.
- Food is only one part of our health, arguably the most important. But never neglect to get a full night of sleep, exercise daily, live an active lifestyle, constantly learn, surround yourself with positive people, bathe, put natural products on your skin, sweat every day, and spend as much time in nature as possible.
- Most Americans are overfed and nutrient-deficient. The objective is to get the most nutrients while consuming the least calories.
- Based on the geographical region of where you believe your ancestors are from, that's how you should align your diet because that's the most natural diet for your biological system.

Nature

Humans are animals; we are from and interconnected with nature. Everything that comes from nature has a purpose. Therefore, the more aligned we are with nature, our body's systems will operate more efficiently.

- Therefore, not living naturally cause disease. Any exposure to chemicals cause disease. Using any ingredients in your body that don't directly come from the earth causes disease. Taking Pharmaceutical medications destroys your immune system. Because they alter our natural state.
- Processed food: Eating foods out of a laboratory instead of natural foods—causes disease. Because you are eating manufactured food, not foo from God. Our ancestors have never seen Doritos or a processed snack.
- Rhythm: Not being in rhythm, life is a bunch of cycles. Everything in life operates in patterns: our body, the seasons, the stock market, etc. You will never feel fully rested if you don't have a consistent sleep schedule. If you wake up tired, something isn't right.
- Light at night: The moonlight was the only light our ancestors were exposed to artificial light at night causes disease by disrupting our circadian rhythm.
- We are designed to live and thrive in a climate that our ancestors derived from. For example, my ancestors were from a tropical region where vegetation was plentiful. Therefore, a plant-based diet is an optimal diet for me. But white people come from colder climates where they didn't have vegetation year-round, which forced them to hunt animals.

Process Foods

Food becomes processed once you alter its natural existence. Humans have eaten naturally occurring foods for thousands of years. Therefore, we modify the body's natural state once man transforms foods. When the body is out of balance, you create disease.

Heating

Cooking foods at high temperatures decreases the food's nutrient value, increases trans-fats, and produces advanced glycation end-products (AGEs). Heterocyclic amines (HCAs) and polycyclic aromatic hydrocarbons (PAHs) are cancer-causing chemicals formed primarily from cooking meats.

- Microwaves use electromagnetic radiation to heat foods. Long-term radiation exposure is cancerous.
- Steaming is the healthiest form of cooking and helps foods retain the most nutrients.

Processing Methods

Preservatives

This method preserves food longer than its actual life span. The most common are:

- Sodium chloride derived from salt, Sodium benzoate, and potassium sorbate are synthetic preservatives. They are all used to stop the growth of bacteria, molds, and yeasts on

foods.
- Consuming food preservatives leads to digestive problems due to sensitivities. It throws off the balance of healthy gut bacteria because these chemicals have just been introduced to humans in recent centuries. Nitrites in processed meats (hot dogs and lunch meat) increase cancer risk. Food coloring in foods such as fruit snacks, cereal, and more has been linked to hyperactivity and behavioral issues, particularly in children.

Additives

These are chemicals put in food to improve flavor and appearance. Here are the most common:

- Artificial sweeteners, food coloring, monosodium glutamate (MSG), and xanthan gum are used to sweeten, add color, stabilize the texture, and add flavors.
- Long-term effects of eating food additives are harmful to the body. Monosodium glutamate (MSG) is found mainly in fast food and chips. Consuming large amounts leads to obesity, increases the risk of liver and kidney damage, decreases the brain's functionality, and literally affects every system in the body. Xanthan gum is found in salad dressing, candy, bread, and more. This gum disrupts our gut bacteria. Healthy gut bacteria help us absorb nutrients and aid in digestion. Artificial sweeteners are found in diet soda or sugar-free foods. This chemical elevates blood sugar and adversely affects mood disorders like depression.

Refining

This form of processing involves stripping the most nutritionally essential nutrients from food.

- The most common refined foods are white bread, white flour, and white rice. If a food is white, it likely has no nutritional value. This means you are literally just consuming food to get full; it has no positive effect on your body.
- Removing the bran and the germ from bread to make white bread, which increases unhealthy carbohydrates and decreases fiber. Which raises the odds of diabetes.
- Natural sugar is sugar naturally occurring in foods such as fruit. Compared to refined sugar, which is processed from sugar cane or beets, This is highly addictive and affects every organ in our body. Especially the liver and pancreas. Leading to fatty liver disease and increasing insulin production by the pancreas, which increases the chances of type 2 diabetes.

Circadian Rhythm

This is our 24-hour biological clock. That regulates our processes and patterns as human beings.

- Light: Sun exposure first thing in the morning energizes the body and provides energy. The darkness at night triggers the body to release melatonin, the sleep hormone. Therefore, artificial lights at night disrupt our natural sleep patterns.
- Temperature: Throughout the day, the body becomes active and alert; therefore, the core body temperature rises. In

the evening leading to the night, the body's temperature gradually decreases to promote healthier sleep at lower temperatures at night.
- Meal timing: The body only needs a meal or less daily. The best time to consume a meal is in the middle of the day. So, your body has ample time to digest and repair. When you eat meals late at night, it stops the body from performing necessary functions during sleep.
- Benefits: A consistent sleep schedule with a full night of sleep ensures the body is fully energized daily to perform at its highest state. Eating once daily improves metabolism and allows your body to reap the benefits of fasting daily.

Environment

An underestimated factor influencing our health is the environment. Over countless generations, our ancestors adapted to the climate they inhabited. They acquired knowledge about how to coexist and adapt to their specific geographic region. People with darker skin tones originate from environments with warmer temperatures, while those with lighter skin tones typically have roots in cooler environments.

- For example, when people with less melanin are exposed to the sun for long periods, their skin burns and breaks. The melanin in people with darker skin helps us better absorb the sun, which means we can spend more extended amounts of time in the sun. Conversely, darker skin people are more vitamin D deficient than white people in climates that get less sun.
- Residing in a climate akin to our ancestors allows for better

alignment with our genetic makeup. We genetically adapted to specific regions over thousands of years, influencing physical features, immune responses, and metabolism.
- Eating foods well-suited to the local climate and in season contributes to optimal health. Because you're eating what nature has designed for you to eat.

Research

Starting on a dietary transformation, you must intensely research food and learn how each food affects your health.

- Many individuals lack awareness about their nutritional choices, often consuming foods without comprehending the negative or positive effects of the foods on their body's health. Understand the difference between micro- and macronutrients, vitamins, and minerals.
- Understand that herbs are derived from plants. They serve as remedies to alleviate illnesses and cure diseases. Replacing the need for pharmaceutical drugs.
- Understand the importance of intermittent fasting and that the body only needs one meal or less daily. If obesity puts you at risk of every chronic disease known to man today, why would you risk being overweight by eating multiple meals a day?
- This higher level of consciousness or awareness ensures that the foods you consume provide you with the highest nutritional content to boost your vitality and long-term health.

Animal Based Foods

- Red Meats (Beef, Goat, and Lamb) are high in calories and saturated fat. Red meat increases the risk of heart disease. The only reason to use it is to bulk up and gain weight for sports.
- Poultry (Chicken, turkey): It raises LDL Cholesterol, has high saturated fat, added additives, and carries a lot of bacteria from the harsh conditions that they live in. The only reason to consume it could be as an alternative to beef.
- Pork (Brisket, some ribs, pork chops): Many people don't eat pork but eat red meat; there's not much of a difference in nutritional value. The only reason to consume is to gain weight for sports.
- Shellfish (Shrimp, crab): They have high exposure to toxins and can't efficiently remove toxins from their bodies. The only reason to consume could be a better alternative than non-seafood options.
- Fish (Salmon, tilapia, and snapper): High exposure to Mercury and other toxic chemicals. The only reason to consume it is that it's arguably the healthiest animal-based food.
- Diary (Milk, butter, cheese, and milk): Linked to cancer; increases heart disease; mucus buildup in the body, which leads to lung diseases; and overall weaker immunity. The only reason to consume it is because it's addictive and adds flavor to food.

Results of Animal Based Foods

I refrain from supporting animal-based foods due to their high-calorie content coupled with limited nutritional value. The emphasis on animal-based diets in the U.S. often serves the interests of powerful industries to promote a standard American diet. The profitability of the unhealthy food industry is driven by the low-quality ingredients that trigger cravings and create dependence. This fuels the healthcare sector as people's health deteriorates, leading to an unnecessary reliance on pharmaceutical drugs. This cycle results in physically sluggish and nutritionally deficient beings.

This creates very heavy and low-nutritious human beings. Animal foods are also low in fiber, which causes people to become constipated. Which leads to weight gain as well as colon cancer. Consuming fat and dead animals lead to a sedentary lifestyle and unproductive behaviors. The extreme lack of nutritional value in such diets also negatively impacts mental health and increases the likelihood of depression and anxiety.

Darker-skinned people have physiological traits more attuned to consuming plant-based foods due to our origins in warmer climates with year-round vegetation. Opting for poor-quality animal products ultimately contributes to low-quality health. Low-quality diet equals low-quality life equals low-quality brain function, which prevents optimal performance and keeps you stuck in a non-efficient cycle of life.

Plant-Based Foods

- Fruits (Mango, Melons, Berries): Rich in nutrients, high in antioxidants, low in calories, high in fiber, and have a high-water content. Consume daily in the morning, for snacks, or throughout the day during fasting.
- Vegetables (Zucchini, squash, peppers, and greens): Rich in nutrients, high in antioxidants, low in calories, and high in fiber. Consume daily and add to meals for flavoring. Eat vegetable-based meals for optimal benefits.
- Nuts (Walnuts, Brazil Nuts): High in minerals, protein, and unsaturated fats, they help regulate blood sugar levels. Nuts, seeds, and fruits should be your only snacks.
- Seeds (Pumpkin, Flax, Hemp): High in minerals, protein, and unsaturated fats, they help regulate blood sugar levels. Add to meals to increase nutritional value.
- Legumes (lentils, beans) Lowers LDL cholesterol and are low in fat and high in protein and fiber. Easy base for meals.
- Ancient Grains (Quinoa, buckwheat): High in B vitamins, low glycemic index, and high in fiber. Easy transition from refined grains.
- Cereal Grain (Oats): Promotes healthy gut microbes and is high in polyphenols and minerals. Easy to incorporate into a raw diet.

Results of Plant-Based Foods

Extensive research and scientific findings have unequivocally demonstrated that adopting a plant-based eating style is optimal for humans to live the highest quality of life while preventing and reversing diseases. The essence of this eating style is to eat the most nutrient-dense foods. Plant-based foods are high in fiber, maintaining healthy bowel movements, a healthy gut microbiome, a cleansed colon, and keeping you at your natural weight. They're high in vitamins, which improve cognitive clarity and learning abilities while reducing the risk of anxiety and depression. It's high in essential minerals, which keep your body in balance. They decrease the risk of cardiovascular disease, the number one killer in America, by lowering LDL cholesterol. The antioxidants in plant-based foods help prevent oxidative stress, which prevents cancer. Finally, they help prevent diabetes by regulating blood sugar levels because of their complex carbohydrates. A plant-based eating regime gives you the energy and brain power to live efficiently.

Journey

Consistently make improvements for sustainable, healthy lifestyle habits.

- Diets are pointless. If you plan to temporarily make healthy changes, then plan to revert back to unhealthy ways. That's like learning how to start a business but never starting one.
- The most essential part of any journey is to get started and never quit. I've been on my plant-based journey for 4 years, and I'm still not perfect. But during the journey, I've only progressively became healthier, and life has exponentially improved in every aspect. I realized my goal is to be healthier every day, not a perfect vegan.
- When someone hates on you during your journey, never get angry, but understand that anyone who hates on someone else has their own insecurities to deal with, and realize the

only people who denounce eating healthy are unhealthy people.
- The point of changing to a plant-based eating style is to put the most nutritious foods in your body, not to mimic an American diet.

Change Perspective

Most Americans are addicted to unhealthy foods and the drugs (sugar) and chemicals that are put into the foods that we consume, so you must slowly wean yourself off your addiction. Mine was candy, so I had to find healthier options that gave me the same sweaty feeling as candy. Until the craving was deceased. You must find what works best for you, whether to never have that food or food type again or to slowly cut back. Then, you must demonize that food or drug and understand how it has affected you, how it will continue to affect you, and how it's used to keep your mind opposed. You must change your perspective on eating and understand that the point is to eat to live, not for comfort, enjoyment, or suppressing feelings.

Why Does it Matter?

"It's a lifelong journey" - A bunch of people

THE EFFICIENCY BLUEPRINT

- Understand we are designed to be one with nature.
- Limit process foods.
- Create a schedule that aligns with your circadian rhythm.
- Move to an environment that benefits your health.
- Deeply understand every food that you touch.
- Remember it's a journey not a race

Steps to a New Lifestyle

5

Never Do It Just to Do It

Think before you Act

- Think before you speak or act.
- Read before you think.
- Live in the moment, but plan for centuries.
- It's vital that we are present and enjoying every single moment.
- If you are living in the past, you are stressed. If you're worried about the future, then you're anxious. When you live in the present, you allow yourself to enjoy every single moment.
- If you have a problem fix it if you can't fix it why worry about it?
- Wealth accumulates over time and is measured by time. Rich is strictly calculated on an income basis.
- When establishing a goal, your initial task is to develop a detailed, step-by-step plan outlining the actions required and the time frame to accomplish that goal.

- Without a well-structured plan, a goal remains merely an abstract thought.
- Understand the risk-reward relationship.
- Then consider is this goal worth your time, money, and energy?

Generational Wealth

Live in the moment, but plan for centuries.

- Your wealth is measured by the worth of your assets compared to the debt of your liabilities.
- Financial freedom is measured by how long you can live off your assets without working.
- Being healthy and building wealth utilize the same principle of delayed gratification. You must sacrifice now to succeed later.
- Too many people get caught up in the day-to-day life of surviving, so they never put themselves and their families in a position to thrive.
- Money is a tool that you use to build wealth. The money itself doesn't have any value. It only matters how you allocate the money.

Keep the End Goal in Mind

- Never buy a house just to buy it. It's definitely better to buy than rent if you can afford it. Use real estate to live for free or create a new source of income.
- Never buy a stock just to buy a stock. Buy a company that you're comfortable with helping you build your net worth.

- Never trade an option just to trade an option. Have an exact strategy for how you plan to use it as a new source of income or to build wealth.
- Never buy a bond just to buy a bond. Use bonds to hedge against recessions or as high-yield savings accounts.
- Never work at a job just to work at a job. Use a job to fund your businesses, gain certifications, and build skills that will make you money forever.
- The goal is to use assets to create wealth for generations.

Goals

Every successful person has mastered the art of effectively creating and understanding what they want to accomplish.

- When considering a goal, it's vital to prudently evaluate all available options.
- When pursuing a goal, it's more beneficial to engage with individuals who have already achieved that goal or are working towards the same objective.
- There's no benefit to seeking advice from people who lack experience in that area or who aren't high achievers.
- Once you identify your goal, write it down and keep it somewhere close or somewhere that you can see it every day.
- Meditate and visualize how you will use that goal to improve your circumstances and imagine yourself already accomplishing that goal.
- Change the way you look at yourself. I was wealthy before I had money because I had a wealthy mindset.

Create a Plan

Live in the moment, but plan for centuries.

- Before you start planning, you must clearly define what you want to accomplish with this goal and how to effectively execute it.
- Break the goal into realistic steps or milestones. Use milestones to measure and track your progress.
- Prioritize what tasks are the most important every day.
- As you create a plan, never become too restrictive; stay agile and be able to adjust and maneuver any challenges or roadblocks.
- Make sure your plan is realistic. If you've been eating garbage your whole life, is it sustainable to completely start eating healthy in one day?
- The purpose of a plan is to map out actions and employ them as a roadmap to achieve your objective. Often in life, individuals set goals without proper planning.

Time, Money, and Energy

As you're precisely discovering what goals are the most important to you and how you want to accomplish those goals. Then, determine whether this goal adds the most value to your life. If so, is the time, money, and energy worth sacrificing for this goal?

- Does it make sense to go to a university for 4 years, graduate with $25k in student loans, and get paid $35k a year?
- Does it make sense to dedicate four years of your life to

getting a job that pays $35k a year?
- In both options above, ask yourself, Is this worth my time, energy, or money?
- Usually, younger people have a lot of time and energy but not much money. So, the best thing to do as a young person is to partner with individuals with capital.
- A busy and stable older person might have a lot of money but less time and energy to dedicate to specific goals. Therefore, they partner with people who have time and energy.
- For us individuals blessed with financial means, ample time, and vibrant energy, the objective shifts to skillfully organizing our lives to safeguard and enhance these precious resources.

Risk-to-Reward

Before making any decision, it's vital to know the best and worst things that can come from that decision.

- Make a list of all the downfalls that can occur when you start a new task. Then, create a list of the positive outcomes. Then, ask yourself, Is it worth it?
- Successful short-term swing traders put themselves in the highest-probability trades possible. Why? Because the reward outweighs the risk. For example, if you make five times as much profit on your wins compared to your losses, you have to win only two out of nine trades to be profitable.
- If you're starting a company and all you need is $300 worth of supplies to make $300 a month each year, Then, for most entrepreneurs, that is worth the risk for the reward.
- Is this risk worth the reward? It takes 3 seconds to kill

someone, the killer then spends their life in prison if they got caught. Then, is that risk worth the reward? Absolutely not.
- Is it worth having a kid with a person you barely know? Hell no.

Why Does it Matter?

"Poor people live day to day. Rich live year to year. Wealthy people live generation to generation " - A few different people

Task / Goal	Duration / Timeline	Value / reward	Obstacles / Risk
Write a book about self discipline to help people create efficiency in their life as well as open up their mind to realized that they are powerful enough to create the life that they want.	Short end: 1 month Date: August 1st. Late end: 2 months Date: August 25th invest fest.	1. Help people become more discipline to achieve their goals, find their purpose, and become more conscious 2. Create a framework. 3. Create intellectual property 4. Keep myself accountable	1. No one applies the principles from the book. 2. I could have been spending this time in a more profitable way. 3. The longer it takes the less time I'll have to just write because referring schedule.

Goal Table

6

I Don't Have Problems

Perception

- Everything in life happens for us not to us.
- There's no good or bad in life, just a bunch of trade-offs.
- When faced with unforeseen circumstances, you have the choice to view these events as problems or as opportunities. By considering all challenges as chances for learning rather than stress-inducing issues, you allow yourself to embrace each situation with optimism and a clear mind instead of approaching it with a clouded perspective.
- I don't have problems; I never stress, and I don't worry. Because I have a profound understanding that I can only control how I react to situations and not the situations themselves.
- If you can't control the weather, why worry about it? Just be prepared for it.

Life is as Good or Bad as you Make It.

Your perception of the world is the only way you can ever see the world. Therefore, if you think life stinks, you will find the worst in every situation. Opposed to an optimistic person who finds the light in every situation.

- There are just trade-offs in life. Good and bad is based off of your belief system.
- If I'm around five millionaires, I can start believing I'm a millionaire because that's who I'm around and what I see everyday.
- Watching the news every day can lead you to think that everything in the world is evil and that the place you live in is much worse than it is.
- Our words and thoughts control our reality. I'm a highly efficient, prosperous, healthy, wealthy divine being. Nothing terrible has ever happened to me.
- The words we use shape our reality for example, "Everything I've ever experienced has been uniquely designed to help me grow and develop into my highest state. I'm the most disciplined person I know. I'm a winner; I can't lose, not because I'm perfect but because I understand that we accomplish whatever we focus our energy on."
- You are what you think you are; once you tell yourself something enough, you will believe it.

Pessimism (Loser Mindset)

Pessimistic people are losers. How could you constantly win if you find the worst in every situation? Unsuccessful people have a lot in common.

- Complain: They tend to complain without changing their circumstances.
- Problematic: Whenever someone tells them about an idea, they always think of why it won't work.
- Lack of willpower: Unsuccessful people have a habit of giving up.
- Self-doubt: They tend not to believe in themselves. How could anyone believe in you if you don't believe in yourself?
- Fake Perfectionist: Unsuccessful people wait for the "perfect timing" instead of just getting started. Have you ever met someone who was supposed to move states or return to school for years?
- Scared to take risk: All unsuccessful people are stuck in a bubble and scared to take the risk to get out of it.

Optimism (Winner's Mindset)

Your likelihood of winning significantly increases when you believe you will succeed. We must learn how to use the immense power of our minds to turn our thoughts into reality.

- "I win in every situation; I don't have problems." I say this very often because if something doesn't go in my favor, I still find the best that came out of that situation, which means all I can ever do in life is learn or acquire new skills.

- I don't have bad days. I never make comments like, "Today was a bad day." I never had a day when everything went wrong. You can find something to be happy about daily if you allow yourself to.
- I can't lose. I understand that life is just a series of trade-offs. There really isn't a right or wrong. Therefore, whatever you believe is true. So why not walk around with a winner mentality? Kobe Bryant only thought about winning. That's why he's a winner.

Successful People

Successful people have commonalities. The only thing you must do to be successful is mimic a successful person's habits. Many people want to mimic results, but you can't mimic the results without the work. Habits led to results. Common traits are:

- Vision: You must be able to visualize yourself accomplishing everything you want to achieve.
- Discipline: What is discipline? Discipline is having control over your mind and habits. It takes focus to complete any task.
- Determination: Regardless of what obstacles you face, you have to know you're going to win.
- Learning: Every single successful person loves and understands the importance of continuous learning.
- Versatile: Being able to adapt to changing environments is everything in life.
- Networking Skills: High achievers understand you go further in life with a team.

Winner's Language

As a winner, I talk like a winner. As a successful person, I speak like a successful person. As a king, talk like a king. As a god, I speak like a god. As a high achiever, I talk like a high achiever.

- I'm not average, so why would I talk like an average person? I'm not a loser, so why would I talk like one? I'm not broke, so I don't speak like a broke person. I'm not from Europe, so why would I talk like I'm from Europe?
- Language is everything. Words are spells; you can tell how people feel and think based on their terms and language.
- It only takes one date for me to tell if a woman is a wife. Just by the level of conversation and the way that they speak about life. It's easy to lie but hard to fake who you are.
- Does it make sense to say negative or derogatory things about you, your family, or your race? Instead of saying negative things, why not give constructive criticism and teach people how to improve?

Why Does it Matter?

"What are the benefits of finding the negative in every situation?" - James Hardy

"let's get money together"	"I can't do this"
"How can I help you"	"If it's not one thing it's another"
"Let's make today better than yesterday"	
	"I hate this job"
"What else can I do to improve"	"I just woke up and my day is already ruined"
"I just get money and travel"	"I don't like people"
"Let's just enjoy ourselves"	"I gotta wait to get paid"
" I just learned…"	

Winner Vs Loser Mindset

7

Experience Everything

Expand

Never miss an opportunity. It never hurts to learn something new. Exposure leads to expansion. Our experiences help shape our reality. If a person lives in one city and doesn't travel, how could you blame that person for having a trapped mindset? They have only experienced one small part of life. Some small-minded people look down on their own people. Imagine being so brainwashed that you belittle your own people. Imagine having an inferior mindset where you put another race above your own. Imagine being black in America, living in one neighborhood your whole life, and making comments like "Black people are poor" or "Black people are violent." How could that person possibly know if they lived in one neighborhood their whole life? Imagine making comments about a country you've never been to. Imagine never experiencing how it feels to live a healthy life. I can't imagine any of that.

Exposure Leads to Expansion

The only thing that separated me from my peers was being exposed to black wealth and seeing firsthand the diversity within my race. From that second on, I knew I was unstoppable. Because I realized media was used to keep our minds inferior.

- Experiences help destroy the limits of your reality. Imagine only ever seeing one way of life; that's all you know.
- There's a difference between someone who has never left their home state and a person who has traveled the world.
- There's a difference between someone who has worked at one company their whole life and someone who has tried to create five businesses.
- There's a difference between someone who sits at home all day and a person who goes to productive events multiple times a week.

Experiences

What are the benefits of experiencing more than your daily routine?

- Learning yourself: New experiences help you learn about yourself. You must continuously seek out and try new things to discover what works best for you. How fulfilling is going to work and then getting off to watch TV and scroll social media almost every day?
- Perspective: Traveling and meeting people allow you to gain new perspectives. The more people you meet, the easier it is to understand life. You have a better understanding of why

people do what they do or how they think.
- Creativity: Experiencing new parts of life helps open your brain to allow you to think beyond the small box that most people live in.
- Opportunities: Every single person you meet is an opportunity to change your life. Because they can have information that can take your life to the next stage:
- Happiness: Engaging in unusual activities and venturing into unfamiliar situations triggers the release of dopamine in the brain, contributing to feelings of increased happiness.

Why Does it Matter?

"Experiencing new experiences is a form of learning." - James Hardy

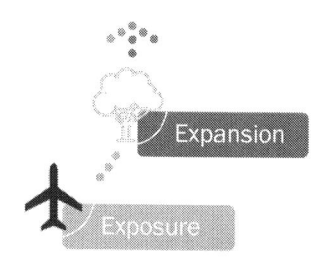

Exposure Leads to Expansion

8

When You Spend You Lose

Don't Spend but Invest

Literally every single dollar that you spend without writing it off, earning some reward from it, or building your credit, you're losing. And by losing, I mean you're not creating wealth, building your credit, or earning anything; you're just becoming more broke.

- Never just spend cash; there's no benefit to that. Use a credit card to earn points and build your credit.
- What's the point of buying something that doesn't produce a return? If it doesn't make you money, don't buy it.
- Instead of just spending money to spend money, create a business that allows you to write off your business expenses to lower your taxable income.
- Imagine living paycheck to paycheck. Imagine setting up your life to spend all your money every time you get paid. I can't imagine.

Why Does it Matter?

"If it doesn't make you money don't buy it." - Dom Kennedy

- Before you start investing, you must be able to manage your own finances.
- Below is an illustration that shows you how to manage your finances like a

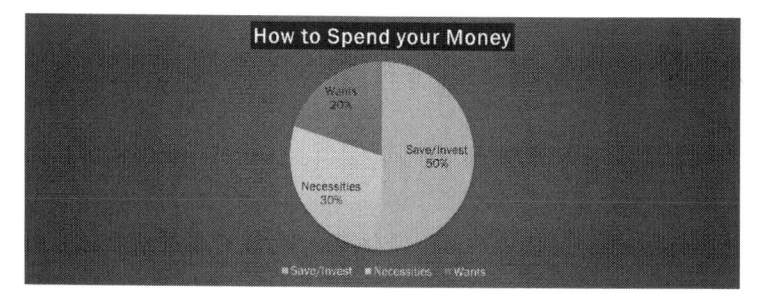

Money Management Chart

9

Wealthy Before Money

Wealthy Mind

I started calling myself wealthy when I was in college and became financially literate. I didn't have much money, but I understood how to create wealth. Wealth is a mindset. All wealthy people know you must sacrifice something now to create more later. For example, instead of watching a new TV show, I'm going to read about how to make more money. I set up my life so that every part and aspect of it centered around investments. Every bill that I pay is an investment. It's more important to have a wealth mindset than it is to have a lot of money. You can have a lot of money but still have a poverty mindset. When you are in poverty, it's hard to think about how to set up the best life for your kids. But when you are living in financial abundance, it is elementary to keep thinking and learning new ways to save your money and help grow it for generations.

Everything's an Investment

Something is only a scam if you lose. Wealthy people have mastered the art of using money to make more money. Below are ways to create wealth.

- Stocks: You buy quality businesses at a fair or undervalued price and just let them grow.
- Real Estate: Buy a home, rent out the other rooms, and live for free.
- Cars: Buy a car and rent out the car to pay for the car note.
- Life Insurance: Use permanent life insurance to turn yourself into a bank; you're able to borrow from your own insurance for other investments.
- Health Savings Account: Contribute tax-free money and withdraw the funds without tax penalty as long as it's for medical expenses or if you are over the age of 65.
- Certificate of Deposits: Use these fixed-term saving accounts to gain higher interest on your money.

Why Does it Matter?

"Money is a tool to use to create wealth" - A lot of financial literate people

THE EFFICIENCY BLUEPRINT

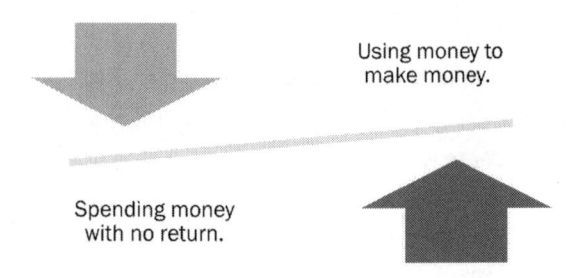

Using money to make money.

Spending money with no return.

Money Options

10

It's a Journey

Get Started

Just get started; you have to take 1 step before you take 5 steps. You can literally close the book and start right now.

- Imagine never getting started because you were waiting for the perfect moment.
- Timing is essential, but getting started is even more critical. The best time to start investing is today.
- Persistence: You never die until you give up. The day you stop growing, you start dying.
- Portfolio: Wealth is created from a portfolio, not a deal.
- Fasting: Fasting heals everything. When you fast, you give your body a chance to reset. You allow your body to focus on recovering and growing.
- Trauma: Revisit every single significant moment in your life, recognize it, and accept it. You can't change it; it's essential to identify where your weaknesses derive from.

Persistence

- To create a successful business, you don't have to offer the best product; you just have to be persistent. For example, McDonald's & Walmart don't have the highest quality products, but they are two of the greatest companies in the world.
- It's better to be determined than it is to be just motivated. Because if you're only motivated, you will only perform while you're motivated. But if you're persistent, you will accomplish your goals regardless of the hurdles.
- If it's not worth putting all your energy into something, it's not worth doing. When you fully dedicate yourself to a task, you will outwork most people because most people never develop the skill of determination. The system is designed for most people to be average, so once you dedicate yourself to being exceptional, you automatically put yourself in the class of the elite.
- Your business never fails until you stop trying. You don't need a great company to succeed; you must be persistent. The average profit margin in the S&P 500 is around 10% over the last 5 years.

Portfolio

A portfolio is an accumulation of assets. On the journey of structuring a portfolio, let one investment lead to the next investment.

- As you build wealth and get closer to financial freedom, it's mandatory that you understand how to create, manage, and grow portfolios.

- It's practical to think of your health as a portfolio; the more time you dedicate to your portfolio (health), the better results you get.
- Reinvesting is essential to growing your portfolio; continuously reinvest the gains or profits from your business, stock, etc., and reinvest them into the portfolio.
- Managing risk is critical for any portfolio to effectively grow. As a short-term trader, you keep a profitable portfolio by managing your win-to-loss ratio instead of chasing gains.

Fasting

Fasting heals everything related to our health.

- It allows our body to reset and return to its healthy balanced state.
- When you eat meals less than 3 hours or so before bed, your body focuses on digesting instead of rejuvenating.
- When you fast, you use your body's fat for energy, which means you lose fat and retain muscle.
- Fasting reduces inflammation, elevated blood sugar and blood pressure levels, cholesterol levels, and any other elevated factor that gives us disease.
- Fasting increases the production of brain-derived neuropathic factors, which allows the brain to operate more efficiently.
- Fasting is a spiritual practice in every religion. Fasting is food for the soul. When you deprive yourself of a perceived necessity creates a deeper level of discipline.

Trauma

Understanding why you feel and act the way you do is essential on your health journey. How can you fix a leak if you don't know where it is?

- Revisit your past, address every traumatic memory in your life, and identify how that the situation has changed or shaped you.
- Study your parents to understand where you get some of your habits, traits, and thoughts. Analyze their strengths and weaknesses. Apply your strengths to your life and leave the weaknesses behind.
- Learn how to be mindful in every situation, which means always being fully aware of your emotions and behaviors. When you're mindful, you give yourself the opportunity to process your feelings and express those emotions.

Why Does it Matter?

"Focus on the journey and not the end goal" - A few people

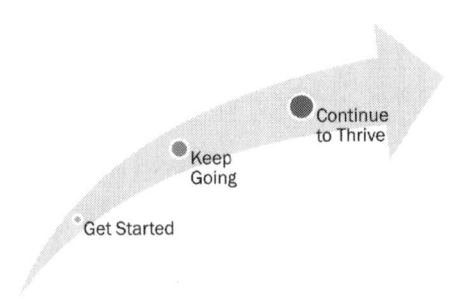

Journey not a Race

11

Pay Attention to What Pays

Habits

Every exceptionally successful individual possesses a unique caliber of concentration. They understand how to gracefully utilize their time to consistently generate value.

- Laziness is a sin. There's no benefit to being lazy. Lazy people are just waiting to die.
- Instead of watching TV, read books to educate yourself.
- Instead of listening to music while working or driving, listen to podcasts or educational documentaries.
- Instead of using social media to be entertained, use social media to gain a larger audience, gain influence, or make money.
- Instead of watching the current and local news, watch the business news so you understand what companies to invest in.
- Instead of doing nothing with your free time, earn a certifi-

cation.
- Instead of gossiping about people, brainstorm solutions to empower them.
- Instead of complaining about a job, start thinking about how you can create work for others.
- Instead of just working for a paycheck, work a job that allows you to gain skills that will help you make money forever.
- Instead of getting up and checking your phone, get up and meditate.
- Instead of paying attention to who celebrities' date, focus on your relationship.
- Instead of using your phone to be entertained, use it as a tool to make your business more efficient.
- Instead of judging someone, teach them.
- Instead of arguing in a relationship, communicate until you have an understanding.
- Before asking someone if they have seen or read some content, ask yourself if this content adds value to their life.

Why Does it Matter?

"Instead of focusing on non-beneficial content that doesn't produce a return on investment for your time, focus your energy on developing yourself and race." - James Hardy

"What you do frequently becomes your frequency " - 19 Keys

PAY ATTENTION TO WHAT PAYS

Utilizing Time	Wasting Time
Creating	Complaining
Reading	Watching non-education television
Promoting your business on social media	Scrolling social media with no purpose
Listening to a podcast / YouTube video	Listening to derogatory music
Working out	Just chilling
Earn a certification	Just chilling
Talk to someone that helps your grow	Talking to negative people
Learning from successful black people	Watching uneducated black people

Time / Value Table

12

Stop Doing too Much

One Goal at a Time

- Instead of mindlessly trying every new trendy thing, allow yourself to fully devote all of your energy to accomplishing one achievement at a time.
- It is more efficient to accomplish 100% of five goals than 10% of 10 goals.
- When you concentrate on one assignment at a time, you allow yourself to complete each task distraction-free without getting overwhelmed.
- Your success rate is higher when you focus on one objective. It's easier to be a guru in one subject than to be excellent in four different subjects.
- Your attention to detail is more potent when you complete one task at a time. Start by choosing the highest-priority task and completing that task first.
- When you focus on one person in a relationship, it's easier to satisfy and give your entire self to that person instead of

dealing with multiple people.
- Imagine always having a new idea but never turning those ideas into realities.

Why Does it Matter?

"You're able to produce better results when you fully engage in one task at a time" - James Hardy

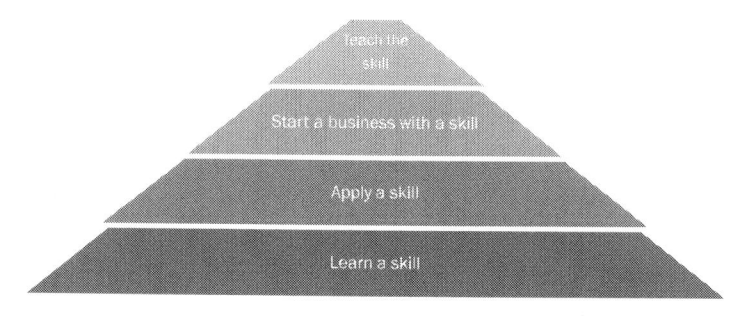

One Goal at a Time

Final Words

- It's not OK to have kids without properties.
- It's not OK to have sex with every person we think we have a connection with.
- It's not OK to drink every weekend.
- It's not OK to not have a business.
- It's not OK to only have 1 or 2 streams of income.
- It's not OK to not reproduce to carry on our legacy.
- It's not OK to be broke.
- It's not OK to be financially illiterate.
- It's not OK to smoke weed every day.
- It's not OK to not work out.
- It's not OK to be fat.
- It's not OK to eat to feed our kids fake food.

If you took the time to read this book, then you've already started to invest in yourself. If you took some things personal, that's even better. Get real with yourself and the people around you; everything isn't OK in life. But we weren't taught these things, and our peers don't hold us accountable, so I don't judge anyone. I've never, in my life, read a book and didn't apply any knowledge from the book to my life. Say you can only apply one principle that is better than zero at this point in your life. Every day is an opportunity to grow, learn, and get better. But hold yourself accountable, continue to thrive, and strive towards the finish line. This book isn't to make money; I make a lot of money. This book is to help the people close to me understand that everything starts from within, and the only way to change that is to dive within.

Why Does it Matter?

"This book is only significant if you want to harness the power to create and shape your own life. But if you're content with just working and surviving then it doesn't matter" - James Hardy

About the Author

I want to share the principles that have led to structured systems that have created efficiency in every aspect of my life. These principles have allowed me to become a 6-figure earner at 23. Then, at 24, I started two businesses and bought my first home. Now, at 25, I am an author with more books coming soon, living bill-free from my investments, and creating six income streams. Currently, structuring my life to start two additional businesses in the next six months. As well as maintaining exceptional health and happiness by being in total control of my time. I can spend time with my family, travel, and constantly experience new thrilling experiences. I can try business ventures at my own discretion and not stress about the time or money involved. This book allows you to add principles to your life that create efficiency. These principles create structure in your life and teach you how to become more disciplined. Self-discipline is about controlling your actions and emotions to craft your desired future. It took me 25 years to write this book and 1 month to structure and publish it with insights from 40 books. This is a book of action, not a story of my life; these are actionable principles to apply to your life. The point of view is written by an African American male that lives in America.

Made in the USA
Columbia, SC
06 February 2025